CABARETS
OF
DEATH

Cabarets Of Death by Mel Gordon
Edited and designed by Joanna Ebenstein

First published by Strange Attractor Press 2024
Text © The Authors 2024

ISBN: 9781907222269

Strange Attractor Press
BM SAP, London,
WC1N 3XX, UK

www.strangeattractor.co.uk

Distributed by The MIT Press, Cambridge, Massachusetts.
And London, England.

Printed and bound in Estonia by Tallinna Raamatutrükikoda.

CABARETS OF DEATH

VISITING HELL, HEAVEN AND NOTHINGNESS IN 19TH CENTURY PARIS

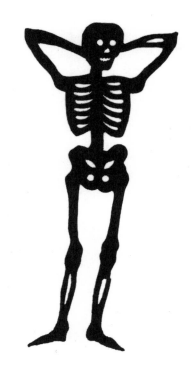

BY MEL GORDON

EDITED BY JOANNA EBENSTEIN

To Joanna Ebenstein,
the Morbid Anatomy Princess

TABLE OF CONTENTS

EDITOR'S INTRODUCTION

Mel Gordon was a rogue scholar. He used the methods of social science to investigate—with great intelligence, vast erudition and an unflagging curiosity—the things we were told not to look at, things not fit for polite conversation, things deemed beneath the dignity of our attention. He lovingly resurrected lost histories of sexuality, perversion and death through intensive research and incredible images with wit, warmth, and exceptional storytelling. He was both a glitteringly brilliant researcher and a trickster working with what others often considered to be low culture at a very high level.

I discovered Mel's work through *Grand Guignol: Theatre of Fear and Terror* (1988), his highly illustrated ode to a 19th century Parisian theater, serendipitously found on a shelf at my local public library. My California suburban, history loving teenage self had never seen anything like it. I spent hours poring over this book, which unearthed for me a macabre and largely forgotten historical moment that seemed too good to be true, with droll, painstakingly researched text and dozens of elegant and often shocking images.

It was hard to know what to make of it. Was this a serious history book? A tongue-in-cheek art project? *Both?*

In the years that followed, I devoured Mel's other books, which wielded a similar approach to similar forgotten (or shame-facedly buried) moments in Western history. There was *Voluptuous Panic: The Erotic World of Weimar Berlin,* a visually-rich deep dive into the sexy cabaret culture of Weimar Berlin, complete with a glossary of contemporary slang for preferred sexual partners, and a list of places different types of prostitutes would solicit for clients. There was also *Horizontal Collaboration: The*

Erotic World of Paris, 1920-1946, a book about the surprisingly rich world of pre-WWII Parisian brothels, one of which even had a playroom stocked with the latest imported toys to keep clients' children happy. Others included *The Seven Addictions and Five Professions of Anita Berber: Weimar Berlin's Priestess of Depravity* and *Erik Jan Hanussen: Hitler's Jewish Clairvoyant.* Another noteworthy title was *Siegel and Shuster's Funnyman: The First Jewish Superhero, from the Creators of Superman,* which introduced us to the *Badkhin,* the traditional Jewish insult artist whose job it was to make people cry at weddings—the genesis, in Mel's opinion, of what we now call Jewish humor. Through all of these books, Mel demonstrated that serious history could encompass literally any topic, and that it could also be, at the same time, scholarly, provocative, informative, artistic, sexy, accessible, inspiring, and most of all, *fun.*

I met Mel in 2010, when I invited him to give a lecture at my newly established Morbid Anatomy event space. This encounter quickly led to a series of collaborations. Over time, Mel became a friend, a colleague, and a beloved mentor. He was delighted by Morbid Anatomy, an institution that, he would laughingly say, "thumbed its nose at mortality."

Mel himself always seemed to be laughing at death. He refused to live small. He worked hard (publishing eight books and leaving several—including this one— unfinished at his death) and played hard (when I asked him how he managed to be so prolific, he replied "I only let myself smoke when I write"). His Port Richmond home doubled as a museum and research library, stuffed full of books, posters, and ephemera, which he accessed via a unique and painstakingly organized system of notation. Upon arrival, you would be greeted with an aphrodisiac drink, a relic from his theatrical production *Dr. Magnus Hirschfeld's Museum of Sexology*: a recreation of the infamous, Nazi-destroyed Weimar sex-club-cum-museum founded by the gay Jewish sexologist Dr. Magnus Hirschfeld, the so called "Einstein of Sex." The production, for a variety of complicated reasons, ended prematurely, which bankrupted Mel. This, he told me with a mischievous smile, was why he started writing books; it was a way he could repackage all the rare material culture he had collected for the production and pay back his creditors.

For all the surface glibness of Mel's work, it is serious stuff, based on deep, original research, following his own particular methodology and his social science training. His rule—which he taught his students as well—was to disregard all received knowledge. One must start from scratch, reading contemporary newspaper and magazine articles, and studying the material culture related to the topic (his books were always richly illustrated with images that he had discovered over the course of his research). If possible, you must find and interview the people who had actually been there—or those who *knew* those who had been.

Mel tirelessly scoured eBay, shops, and private collections in search of artifacts which everyone but he was certain had been irrevocably lost. He was blessed with a preternatural serendipity in this department, somehow unearthing scratchy black and white footage of Soviet constructivist productions from the 1910s, or Anita Berber Berlin cabaret dances from the 1920s, boasting names like "Cocaine" or "Morphium." Mel would casually share these treasures, like a magician pulling back a curtain, during his many unforgettable lectures. As they flickered silently before our eyes, the audience would be spellbound, in awe at the forgotten history being conjured for us.

Mel was also funny, charming, witty, and the best storyteller you ever met. He had a gift for weaving together research and imagery into dazzling productions that enthralled, amazed, inspired, and delighted, while at the same time imparted knowledge. The histories that Mel unfolded—in understated sentence after sentence, in his books and in lectures—defied belief. But the joke of it was that they were true— *always* true—no matter how unlikely it seemed. Unearthing such outlandishly amazing but absolutely true histories and their artifacts was among Mel's special gifts.

I imagine that Mel Gordon is laughing at death right now. Of all the people I know, he is the one who had—or so I would hazard from what I knew of the man, and the stories I heard at his funeral—the fewest regrets about a life unlived upon his death bed. His zest and energy for a deeply-felt, connected, rich life lived entirely on his own terms—alive with passion, unflagging curiosity, a sense of adventure, and a drive towards meaningful work—continues to be an inspiration.

I like to imagine that somewhere, Mel is watching us still here on earth, and getting a kick out of the absurdity of it all, Laughing at the fact that some of his collections went to the Harry Ransom Center at the University of Texas Austin after his death, and he got a laudatory obituary in *The New York Times*.

I also hope it would delight him to know that this book came to be, so that he could continue to engage us with his warm, erudite, brilliant, and fun work about life, sex, death and fun from beyond the grave.

—JOANNA EBENSTEIN, Founder and Creative Director of Morbid Anatomy

ABOUT THE STRUCTURE OF THIS BOOK

The book you hold in your hands was a project Mel and I planned to produce together. Sadly, Mel died before it was completed. His nephew, Maer Ben-Yisrael, and the Mel Gordon estate kindly gave us their blessing to bring this edition to fruition.

Because this is the first posthumous Mel Gordon book, and thus a memorial of sorts, I invited some of those who knew and loved the author to say a few words about him: Jim Hoberman is a journalist, film critic, author, and longtime staff writer for *The Village Voice*; Atay Citron is Professor and Chair of the Theatre Department of Israel's University of Haifa.

A NOTE ON IMAGE QUALITY

Mel Gordon was a genius at finding images no one else could. Not all of these were of the best quality. We have done the best we could with the images provided, which often were from popular sources and not very fine to begin with. We hope you will overlook these issues, and find the charm in the images that we believe shines through despite their imperfections.

FOREWORD BY J. HOBERMAN

Mel Gordon was one of the world's great gleaners. How did he know so much? Where did he find things and find things out? When I think of Mel, I think of him spinning some incredible sounding, if not totally outlandish yarn, with a matter-of-fact delivery and a mysterious half smile. I couldn't quite believe him but, inevitably, the fantastic stuff he discovered or experienced was absolutely true.

Modernist sideshows were Mel's forte. His interests included, but were not restricted to, radical stage directors and theorists (notably the Russians, Stanislavsky and Meyerhold), left wing Yiddish theater (I think he interviewed every surviving member of the ARTEF), and something he called "fascist love cults," as well as outré communist artists (Nikolaï Foregger comes to mind), Weimar bad girls (Anita Berber and Valeska Gert), Grand Guignol, Jewish humor (ranging from medieval *badkhonim* to the short-lived comic book *Funnyman*), 80s performance art, and the notion of bad acting. He created archives and wrote books on some of these subjects and, to our loss, left others unfinished. (His methodology, I've been informed, was to spend years on research and weeks on the actual writing.)

A showman and master of the PowerPoint lecture, as well as an underground historian in the sense that R. Crumb and S. Clay Wilson were underground cartoonists, Mel gave his copiously-illustrated books titles that were frankly sensational, particularly once he found a simpatico publisher, Feral House. Who could resist *Erik Jan Hanussen: Hitler's Jewish Clairvoyant; Anita Berber: Weimar Berlin's Priestess of Depravity* or, Mel's lone book to be reviewed in *The New York Times, Grand Guignol: Theatre of Fear and Terror?* Not I.

Mel was a maverick scholar. Generous with his ideas and collected material, he was one of the most informative, least academic professors I've ever known. Evidently, his colleagues thought so too. He told me that he was denied a promotion at the University of California Berkeley as a result of publishing his astonishing coffee table book *Voluptuous Panic: The Erotic World of Weimar Berlin*—not coincidentally one of his several projects that attracted the attention of Hollywood movie-makers who, no less than Mel's fellow PhDs, ultimately found his thinking too far-out to assimilate.

Cabarets of Death was a spin-off from Mel's equally amazing sequel to *Voluptuous Panic, Horizontal Collaboration: The Erotic World of Paris, 1920-1946*. In the course of researching French brothels, he collected data on three Grand Guignol theme-park restaurants operating in Montmartre during the first half of the 20th century. The only previous English-language reference I've been able to find regarding these bizarre institutions is in the final paragraphs of a scholarly essay on the origins of late 19th century French *cabarets artistiques*. (Not surprisingly, the essay, by John Houchin, a former student of Mel's at NYU, was published in *The Drama Review* during the period that Mel was the journal's associate editor and encouraged many such excavations of theater's repressed history.)

Variously ghoulish, blasphemous, and outrageously tawdry, the Cabarets of Death represented the commercialization of the *cabarets artistiques*. Salacious and sophisticated entertainment, they were designed to titillate tourists—part degenerate Folies Bergère, part living French postcards, part Georges Méliès techno-conjuring show, an adult Euro-Disney *avant la lettre* that might have been invented to serve as grist for Mel's mill.

—J. HOBERMAN, New York City

FOREWORD BY ATAY CITRON

Mel Gordon, my friend and in more than one way my mentor, was telling me about the cabarets of death in one of the last conversations we had at his home near Berkeley, California. He was already quite sick and weak at that time, but as always, when he talked about one of his research projects, he was animated, his voice strong, his words flowing rapidly, and that familiar twinkle in his eyes rekindled behind the round glasses.

When he talked about the cabarets of death, it was as if he was sharing precious secrets with me, as he had done in the past when he was exploring Yiddish theater in Soviet Birobidzhan, or when he discovered that Stanislavski found the key to his system when he was practicing yogic meditation with his teacher, Sulerzhitsky, a stage hand at the Moscow Art Theatre. The amazing findings—always based on solid evidence—were presented with the bravura of a stage magician presenting a new trick. It was the same when he was lecturing to theater students and when he addressed a large crowd in a museum, introducing his reconstruction of scenes from a Meyerhold production, or presenting the incredible story of Erik Jan Hanussen, Hitler's Jewish Clairvoyant. Those secrets were hidden from other scholars, Mel contended, because academics tend to repeat what they read in other people's books instead of searching for primary materials.

For Mel, primary materials were essential for research. He spent a fortune purchasing memorabilia, old popular magazines, brochures, diaries and esoteric film footage. He traveled across the Atlantic to interview old actors who in their youth worked with one great director or another and were ready to reminisce and to show him their notes and photos of the old days. In other words, Mel knew things that others didn't because for him research was detective work, and what he discovered often changed the perspective on a particular subject or at least added a new, fresh point of view that made cultural phenomena appear more complex and interesting.

The book you are holding now is an example of a process that would normally begin with Mel stumbling upon some hazy information about an extraordinary, sometimes bizarre phenomenon—in this case, the Montmartre cabarets of death, which were outstanding even in the cultural landscape of bohemian Paris of the Belle Epoque. Brief mentions of the cabarets of death were made in a few books by other scholars as well as in Mel's own book *Horizontal Collaboration: The Erotic World of Paris 1920-1946* (a sequel to his best-selling book, *Voluptuous Panic: The Erotic World of Weimar Berlin*).

Once Mel's curiosity was aroused, and with it, the desire to know everything about that phenomenon, the hunt for primary materials was launched. Pictures, texts, advertisements, reviews and testimonies were obtained—in recent years, many of them through eBay. Each item offered some detail, like the parts of a puzzle or the shards of an antique vase that the archaeologist has to put together in an attempt to learn something significant about an ancient culture. Mel's broad knowledge of popular entertainment, the history of the avant-garde, and the culture of turn-of-the-century Paris were all recruited for that effort, as well as his creative imagination. As in previous projects, he wished to reconstruct the performances as fully as possible, so that the reader could imagine participating in them. Had he not died in 2018, Mel would have possibly tried to recreate one of those cabarets that allowed spectators to experience death before they actually die.

For quite some time, Mel was talking about his own approaching death. "I have one, maybe two years to live," he asserted when he was visiting me in Israel. I saw no signs of his failing health at the time, but he was apparently correct, even if he lived a little longer than he had predicted. Strangely enough, when he discussed the cabarets of death in the summer of 2017—half a year before he died—neither he nor I associated that form of morbid entertainment with the death that was knocking on his door.

Unfortunately, the book was not published in Mel's lifetime, but thanks to the efforts of his nephew, Maer Ben-Yisrael, the publisher Strange Attractor Press, and his former collaborator on morbid creativity, Joanna Ebenstein, it is in your hands now, and it will take you as close to the actual experience of visiting the cabarets of death as any book can take you.

The cabarets of death were harbingers of what is known today as immersive theater, i.e. performance in which the designed environment envelops the audience in order to create a total experience, and the spectators are encouraged to interact in some way with the setting and the performers. The cabarets of death were original inventions, amalgams of innovative concepts of entertainment, bold entrepreneurship, and an exploration of a subject that was taboo on the one hand, and on everybody's mind on the other. Whereas the originality of those cabarets cannot be disputed, it is also clear that they were part of a long tradition.

The theme of death ignited the creative imagination of humans from prehistoric times. It found expression—and still does—in myths, poetry, literature, visual and performing arts, sacred rituals and popular festivals such as the Mexican *Dia de los*

Muertos (Day of the Dead)—a tradition that goes back to Aztec rituals, which is still celebrated with music and dance, commemorating the deceased of the family by displaying their photos, favorite foods and personal objects on the *ofrendas* (altars) or on their gravestones, and by preparing the *Calaveras*—the colorful, sweet, edible skulls.

In antiquity as well as in modern times, the living arrange elaborate funerary rituals that send the deceased on a journey to another existence. What is that other existence like? We do not know. Where does it take place and how long does it last? The lack of answers to these questions bedevils us.

> …But that the dread of something after death,
> The undiscovered country, from whose bourn
> No traveller returns, puzzles the will,
> And makes us rather bear those ills we have,
> Than fly to others that we know not of?
> —Shakespeare, *Hamlet,* Act III scene 1

The only way to cope with that anxiety is to imagine the afterlife, as Dante did in his *Divine Comedy* (1320), for example. The poetic description of his journey to Inferno, with its nine circles, from there to Purgatorio and its seven terraces, and finally to Paradiso, is so specific and detailed that the reader or the listener is ready to believe in their actual existence. Almost two centuries after Dante, Hieronymus Bosch painted the densely populated heaven and the ominous hell in his fantastic *Garden of Earthly Delights* (1505).

Jewish mystics, too, imagined an afterworld divided into Heaven and Hell, each with seven compartments, and each compartment with a name, a specific character and a function. Earlier still, the Sumerians believed that the souls of the dead journeyed to the demon-populated dark world of Kur, which was ruled by the goddess Ereshkigal. They had to pass through seven gates before they were admitted by the gatekeeper, and once there, they were fed only with dry dust. The ancient Egyptians, the Greeks, in fact all cultures, had their own imagined, theatrical afterlife worlds, populated by angels and demons, and characterized by excessive pleasure and suffering. The experiences of life—the only ones we know—are transported, exaggerated, hyperbolized to create the imaginary worlds of the afterlife. In that sense, the three 19th century cabarets of death in Montmartre went along with the traditional conceptions. Cabaret du Ciel focused on the imagery of Heaven, Cabaret de l'Enfer represented Hell or Inferno, and Cabaret de la Mort, which was later renamed Cabaret du Néant (nothingness), presented a variety of images of the afterlife.

Death itself became a cultural obsession in Europe in the second half of the 14th century, after the Black Death eradicated up to one third of the continent's population. The Black Death, which left no household unscathed, was portrayed in murals and prints in the image of a skeleton, either bare or robed. The skull, its teeth exposed with no lips to cover them, seemed to be smiling a horrid smirk, which was accentuated by the empty eye sockets. That smiling skeleton was dancing with men, women and children as partners. *La Danse Macabre*, the Dance of Death, probably appeared for the first time on a 15th century mural in the Paris cemetery Cimetière des Saints-Innocents. Each of the mural's thirty paintings depicted two male characters being invited to dance with

Death, and each was accompanied by an eight-line satirical verse that was often bold, even risqué. Death as a grotesque caricature in situations characterized by dark humor with erotic innuendos became fashionable in Europe. Basel and Lübeck had their own *Danse Macabre/Totentanz* murals, and although the walls on which they were painted were demolished, their texts and illustrations were copied and preserved in printed books.

The most famous and most influential examples of that tradition are the miniature *Totentanz* woodcuts and the *Totentanz* satirical alphabet by the young Hans Holbein. Both were created in Basel in the early 1520s. They depict Death, the skeleton, playing a trumpet and a drum, coming by surprise to people of all ages and all walks of life—from the Pope to the poor farmer—and inviting them to dance.

Holbein's *Totentanz* illustrations, which were printed and circulated across Europe, inspired generations of European artists and writers. Artists and poets affiliated with the symbolist movement of the second half of the 19th century embraced the *Danse Macabre* and were enthralled with the theme of death. They were also very much involved with the cabaret movement, a fact which, as we shall see, may explain the prevailing presence of that theme in the counterculture of cabaret's early days.

Of the numerous symbolist paintings that were inspired by *Totentanz*, it may be useful to look at two by artists less known than the celebrated James Ensor, Gustav

Opposite page: Physician and Suitor invited by Death for a dance, from a printed version of the Saint Innocents Danse Macabre.

This page: Initial capital letter "A" from Holbein's Dance of Death Alphabet.

Klimt or Edvard Munch. *Self-Portrait with Death as Fiddler* by the Swiss artist Arnold Böcklin was completed circa 1872. In the foreground, a concerned yet focused and determined artist seemingly looking at his reflection in the mirror in order to paint his self-portrait. In the background, but extremely close to the artist's left ear, Death—the familiar grinning skull, the violin bow held by a skeletal hand—is playing the *Totentanz* tune, and apparently, Death is what the artist really sees when he looks in the mirror.

In *The Garden of Death* (1896), the Finnish symbolist artist Hugo Simberg painted three figures of Death tending to a garden with young plants and flowers. With grim reapers as gardeners, one cannot but wonder what it is that grows in those decorated boxes.

The symbolist fascination with death marked the history of

cabaret. The first *Cabaret Artistique,* founded by Rodolphe Salis in November 1881 in Montmartre, was called *Le Chat Noir* (The Black Cat) as an homage to Edgar Allan Poe's short horror story by the same title. The tale is a confession of a psychopath who murdered his wife with an axe and hid her corpse in the brick wall of his basement, together with the black cat that he had blinded earlier with a pocket knife. The story was translated into French by the poet Charles Baudelaire, who idolized Poe and the tormented perversity of his prose.

Death, decay, ennui, alcohol, hashish, opium and sex were the principal themes in Baudelaire's own poems that were collected under the title *Les Fleurs du Mal* (Flowers of Evil, 1875). This scandalous book that had the poet prosecuted and fined for an "offense against public morals" became the inspiration for the symbolist poets Stéphane Mallarmé, Arthur Rimbaud and Paul Verlaine—a group that was proudly carrying the name *Les Poètes Maudits*—the accursed poets, as Verlaine called them in his 1884 essay of the same title. In the poem 'Langueur' (Languor, 1883), which could be perceived as a poetic manifesto of the Decadent Movement in poetry, Verlaine expressed heartache, ennui, feebleness, and a yearning for death, for emptiness or nothingness (*néant*). Rimbaud's 1873 collection of prose poetry was called *Une Saison en Enfer* (A Season in Hell), so it seems that the stage had been set for the cabarets of death about a decade or two before they were founded.

The hub of the *Poètes Maudits* prior to the opening of the Chat Noir was a brasserie at the foot of the Montmartre hill, known as *Le Rat Mort* (Dead Rat Café)—a title reflecting the reversed aesthetics of the symbolists: that which is *mal* (evil) in the eyes of the bourgeoisie, repulsive, and associated with filth and epidemic disease was made spitefully attractive to them, as a joke perhaps—a meaningful joke. It was at Le Rat Mort that the drunk Rimbaud accidentally slashed the thigh of his lover, Verlaine, during a dangerous game with a knife. According to the annals of Montmartre, that was not the single incident of violence in that café, and definitely not in the stormy relations of those two *Poètes maudits*. On another occasion, in a hotel room in Brussels, it was the drunk Verlaine who shot Rimbaud twice, wounding his arm. He was later charged with attempted murder, the charges were reduced to wounding with a firearm, and he was sentenced to two years in prison.

There was also the *Cabaret des Assassins* in Montmartre, decorated with pictures of the famous murderers of the period. It was re-christened as *Au Rendez-vous des voleurs* (The Meeting Place of Thieves), and only later received the name that made it famous for generations: *Le Lapin Agile* (The Agile Rabbit).

Hence, when the cabarets of death opened in Montmartre in 1892, it seemed that the Paris bohemia was well prepared for their opening. A few years later, in 1901, the Montmartre spirit crossed the border to Germany. Munich's leading cabaret, the hub of the Bavarian city's most celebrated poets, named itself *Die elf Scharfrichter* (The Eleven Executioners). Each of its founders created a stage name for himself that was related to death: Balthasar Starr (Balthasar Rigor Mortis), Dionysius Tod (Death), Till Blut (Blood), Frigidius Strang (Hangman's Rope) and so on. Sarcasm, social and political critique were always part of the cabaret, but it is important to remember that what we are discussing here and what this book is about is entertainment. Death and the afterlife appear to be excellent materials for a unique kind of entertainment—the kind which is innovative, theatrical and sometimes also

Facing Page:
Deathcafe.com

philosophical. In fact, before it opened in Paris, the Cabaret du Néant opened in Brussels as *Cabaret Philosophique*.

★ ★ ★

We still die, and most of the time, we still sweep the discussion of death under the carpet. A novelty of our time is Death Café, in which people are invited to talk about their own death in a relaxed atmosphere, over coffee and cake. Death Café was initiated in 2004 as *café mortel* by the Swiss sociologist Bernard Crettaz, with the objective of breaking the "tyrannical secrecy" surrounding the topic of death. Jon Underwood, a British web developer, started Death Café in London in 2011, and promoted it in 66 countries as a framework for open conversations about the end of life. He also created the popular Death Café website that among other things formed a global Death Café virtual community (https://deathcafe.com/).

In German speaking countries, Death Café is known as Totentanz-Café. It offers no dancing or magic tricks, however. It is an intimate social gathering, focusing on verbal intercourse, somewhat like group therapy perhaps, and normally avoiding dark humor. But the imagery one finds in its websites does remind one of the classic *Totentanz*.

—ATAY CITRON, Professor and Chair of the Theatre Department of Israel's University of Haifa

CABARET DU NÉANT

CABARET OF NOTHINGNESS, PARIS, 1892—1956

Early in 1892, Antonin Dorville established the Café de la Mort in Brussels. An illusionist who designed "Black Art" projections for itinerant magic stage shows, Dorville combined the notion of a restaurant as a mortuary with an adjoining room that cast animated facsimiles of decaying human flesh and ghostly apparitions. His sensational locale proved to be a lucrative enterprise but, after a few months, he moved it to 53, Boulevard du Clichy in Paris, renaming it the Cabaret du Néant, the "Cabaret of Nothingness."

Dorville's novel import flourished and, in June 1895, he transferred his commercial undertaking across the street to 34, Boulevard du Clichy, where he added several darkened rooms. It remained in place until 1956.

With Cabaret du Néant's phenomenal growth and playful notoriety came savage criticism from indigenous reviewers, who disparaged its mocking tenor as "morbid and neurotic." Tourists and out-of-towners, relying on word-of-mouth communication, however, flocked to it.

On January 18th, 1896, a replica of the Néant opened in the Casino Chambers on 39th Street and Broadway in New York City. Eschewing its French culinary setting, the Manhattan Néant offered 30-minute walk-throughs from 8pm to midnight for 25 cents. Besides ambulant and disarticulated skeletons, spectators could marvel at the sleight-of-hand projections of blank-faced cadavers and graveyard phantoms. Included in this "Parisian sensation" was the first public exhibition of an X-Ray Machine in North America.

Two months later, Albert A. Hopkins published an illustrated exposé of the Néant's mirror and plate glass optical tricks in *Scientific American* (March 7, 1896). They were all variations of an ingenious technique known as "Pepper's Ghost." Imitations of the Broadway Néant appeared at New England carnivals and fairs around Halloween for several years.

Although French academics and intellectuals generally ignored the Cabaret du Néant in Montmartre, the Surrealists, led by André Breton, conducted sleep experiments in the floor above the restaurant-nightclub in 1920.

CABARET DU NÉANT

BOULEVARD DE LICHY 1892–1946

AREA

18th ARRONDISSEMENT, Montmartre.
Directly across from the Cabarets du Ciel et L'Enfer.

ATMOSPHERE

Even more droll and macabre than L'Enfer: a grisly caricature of Eternal Nothingness. A black-caped croquemort, or pall-bearer, ushers in the curious diners through a sidedoor. The black draping and grotesque positioning of the skeletons on the walls suggest the aftermath of a frightful catastrophe or a dismembering station in a charnel-house. A distinct odor of death hovers.

CLIENTELE

Foreign tourists, especially Germans, who are addressed as "Brother and Sister Coffin-Worms". French provincial couples are sometimes called Maccabées (sailor slang for the lifeless bodies found floating in riverbeds).

DÉCOR

A dim "Room of Incineration" is lighted with wax tapers and a large chandelier devised of three human skulls (including an infant's) and fleshless fingers holding funeral candles. Large, heavy wooden coffins, resting on biers, are set about the room as dining tables. White skulls rest on the coffin-tops. Guests are handed tapers that eerily illuminate their faces when they order.

ENTERTAINMENT

A black-frocked cleric, holding a human leg-bone, reminds the "Coffin-Worms" of their impending doom and reels off the incredible varieties of dissolution that the Grim Reaper has planned for them. While he pontificates about their painful demises, glowing panels of frolicking men and music-hall dancers divulge their worldly futures as hideous skeletal remains. Other objets d'art include a bleeding neck from a guillotined victim and a laughing skull that flies through the air. After this, the monkish MC invites the revelers (for one franc) into the "Tomb of Death." There, in a pitch-dark chamber, the candle-holding patrons watch figures pour out of an upright coffin while a harmonium wheezes an off-key funeral march. One of them is a rosy-faced femme who magically decomposes into a bald and fleshless corpse as she bewails her agonizing fate. Afterwards, a few audience members are led into the trick stage box, transformed visually into their imminent future as emaciated cadavers before their friends, and then restored to their stocky selves. The whole thing lasts about thirty minutes.

EROTIC ENTICEMENT

In a third dank room (another franc, merci), the Graveyard, a female spectator is coerced into sitting in a chair inside another upright coffin. Without any warning, her outer garments seem to vanish and, through a mirror projection, she is made to appear in provocative and revealing underclothing. Of course, the female Worm is unaware of this immodest transformation and blankly stares back at her delighted audience.

FOOD

The morbidly slow waiters are dressed as top-hatted hearse-followers and describe each drink as a deadly contagion: a glass of bock beer is referred to as one microbe of Asiatic cholera; cherry liquor as a malignant cancer; crème de menthe as a dose of TB.

UNUSUAL

When the crowd files out of the Tomb of Death, they are encouraged to drop coins into an inverted skull, which will ensure them of a longer life on this earth.

ALCHOHOLIC DRINKS

Absinthe—"the juice of crushed maggots"
Glass of Alsatian bock beer—"foam from Asiatic cholera germs"
Glass of lager beer—"glass of strychnine"
Cerises à l'eau-de-vie (cherries in alcohol)—"bone marrow from a corpse who died of malignant cancer"
Crème de menthe—"sputum from a TB victim"
Rum cocktail—"pall bearer"
Vermouth—"shot of cholera"
Glass of château la pompe wine—"glass of funeral Parlor"

HORS-D'OEUVRE

Oysters from Ostend—"soft-boned oysters"

FISH

Fish in sauce—"weeping willow"

ENTREÉS-"EXHUMED"

Roast lamb—"tranquility"
Italian macaroni—"one word from cambronne" (shit)
Ox tripe from Lyons—"two death knell tolls"
Cooked potatoes in their skins—"man underground"
Sandwich—"sighs of the dying"

ASSORTED DESSERTS-"ASSORTED DEATHS"

Plate of brie—"pray for him"
Fruit cup—"a hearse"

At the Café du Neant (Café of Nothingness) customers entered a chamber dimly lit by wax tapers suspended on a chandelier composed of human skulls and arms. As the people were ushered in by waiters dressed as undertakers they were seated at tables made of coffins. While they were being attended to, they were free to ponder the images of death, carnage and assassination that adorned the walls. After drinking les microbes de la mort, the customers would be ushered down the "Hall of Incineration" to behold a spectacle of death and decay. A member would be chosen from the audience to be placed in an upright coffin. Using a projected image, glass and mirrors an illusion was cast to make it appear to the crowd as if that person decomposed into a skeleton:

> *"Enter mortals of this sinful world, enter into the mists and shadows of eternity. Select your biers to the right, to the left; fit yourselves comfortably to them and repose in the solemnity and tranquility of death; and may god have mercy on your souls!"* Bohemian Paris of Today *p. 265 (1899)*

There were women who went among these cabarets selling flowers to the patrons. Many were known to sell bouquets laced with cocaine; which were often purchased by a certain sort of "European nobleman." These "gentlemen of leisure" used it to seduce the unsuspecting female, usually from the United States or Great Britain. Amidst the Absinthe, the cocaine, the champagne, the music, the dancing, the frolics and the various other sensual wonders, one partook of the sacraments of the Bohemian mysteries. These initiates were drawn to these night spots to partake of something they imagined to be exotic or ordinarily forbidden to them; or to forget something they wished to leave behind.

"To astonish you, to give you a sensation, to quicken into some sort of action your jaded nocturnal nerves, is the object of all these places." *New York Times* May 14, 1911.

CAFÉ DU NÉANT DIALOGUE

ROOM OF INTOXICATION

Chief Croquemort: Welcome, O weary wanderers into the Realm of Death! Find your way into the mists and shadows of Eternity. Choose your coffin and be seated beside it! May God have mercy on your souls!

Croquemort Waiter: Good evening, Maccabées (Floating Cadavers)!

Bar-Tender: One microbe of Asiatic cholera from the last corpse, one leg of an active cancer, and one sample of our TB germ!

Croquemort Waiter: Drink, Maccabées! Drink these noxious potions, which contain the vilest and deadliest poisons!

TOMB OF THE DEAD

Monk: Beloved Maccabées enter into Eternity, whence none ever return!

O Maccabée, beautiful, breathing mortal, pulsating with the warmth and richness of life, thou art now in the grasp of Death! Compose thy soul for the end!

Ah, ah, Maccabée! Thou hast reached the last stage of dissolution, so dreadful to mortals. The work that follows Death is complete. But despair not, for Death is not the end of all. The power is given to those who merit it, not only to return to life, but to return in any form and station preferred to the old. So return if thou deservedst and desirest.

You have at last arrived at that point in your careers where you are to leave your souls behind you. While we must require thus, yet we are willing that you should be a witness to the process. Is there anyone in this company so sick of existence that he will take his place in the domino-box and undergo immediate disintegration? Have no fear! It is not only perfectly painless but it is the only real state of happiness.

Bid your friends an eternal farewell! Compose yourself and think on higher things. Now step into the wooden overcoat, please. It could not fit you better had it been made to measure! Now the shroud, please! Cover him with it, all but the face. Are you prepared? Die then!

He perishes! May he rest in peace!

Behold annihilation! Weep not. He is in another world.

They've turned him out! Would someone else like to try?

HALL OF SPECTRES

Now, my daughter, what do you desire above everything else? Do not be shy, tell me. How would a fine new dress do? That one you are wearing seems rather plain and shabby, doesn't it? In fact, I am surprised that you should take such a promising position as this before the public in such an unbecoming dress. Come, shall I change it for you? Don't be shy, it can all be done for you in a twinkling. Shall I order a new silk or satin wholly at our expense? There you are!

Left: a panama-hatted Croquemort, or hired pallbearer, ushers in the curious diners:
"Welcome, o weary wanderers, to the realm of death! Enter! Choose your coffin and be seated beside it!"

CABARET DU
NÉANT

64, Boulevard de Clichy (angle de la Rue Coustou)
Montmartre

●

La bouteille de bière .... _____

La bouteille de limonade . _____

Les liqueurs de marques. _____

Le Menu est à l'intérieur

*Right: the morbidly slow waiters are dressed as hearse-drivers
and describe each drink as a deadly contagion.*

"Coffin-Worms, behold the microbes of death! Drink them with resignation!"

Diner des Squelettes

Invitation

—

Frères

il faut

Moult rire !

Enfer et

contre tout

MENU
rédigé pour la faim du monde
d'après l'art d'accommoder les restes

Peaux d'âges
Riz aux larmes (Persil, et cercueil)

Hors-d'œuvre
Peur et raidis verts
Huîtres d'os tendres

Poissons
Sole pleureur - Raie quiem

Enterrées
Grognons aux truffes du Père Ricord
Glas double
Râles en salmis
Veuf à la morgue
Ci-gît got rôti

l'Exhume
Cardons du Poêle
Macabroni italienne
Petits Pois trinaires
Choux-pleurs
Homme de terre en robe de chantre

Bombes Funèbres

—

Décès assortis
Corbillard de fruits
Brie ez pour lui

Bois-son
Château la Pompe Funèbre 1924
Petits verres - Bière garantie 10 ans
Groge Maure

SPECTRE-TRAC CANCER

Le Posthume est de rigueur,
Les invités pouvant être reconduits en voiture à leur dernière demeure.

Small talk …

... and no talk.

The gloomy "room of intoxication" is illuminated with a huge chandelier constructed from human bones and three skulls.

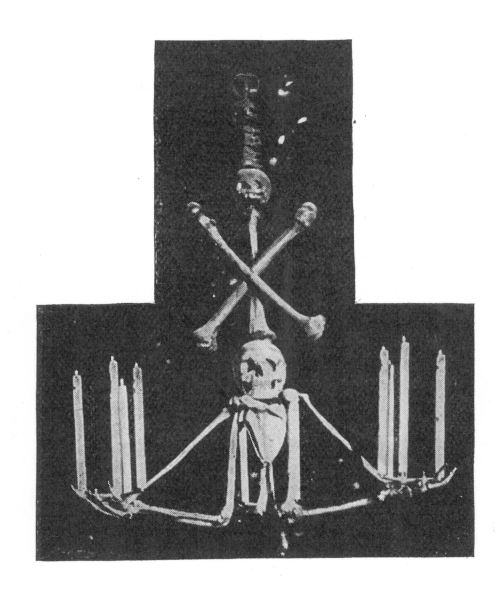

Looking up ...

... and waiting
for the show.

CABARET DU NÉANT - Paris-Montmartre — n° 1. Salle d'Intoxication

Charon, a black-frocked cleric, pressing a thigh-bone against his chest, summons the "Coffin-Worms".

He speaks of their impending doom and reels off the varieties of dissolution that
the grim reaper has planned for them. Their future is invariably eternal nothingness.

While Charon pontificates about their painful demises, glowing panels of frolicking men and music-hall dancers divulge their imminent fates as hideous cadavers.

As the lights are dimmed, a canvas of frolicking lovers reveals their future doom in a graveyard.

The painting of "Pierrot's serenade" illuminates his ultimate demise.

And a picture of the Moulin Rouge orchestra with its unruly guests below also discloses their otherworldly fates.

CABARET DU NÉANT - Paris-Montmartre - n° 1, Salle d'Intoxication

Other objets d'art include a bleeding neck from a guillotined victim and a laughing skull that flies through the air.

The pallbearer encourages a spectator to buy a jeton for the show.

The monkish MC invites the revelers (for ten francs) into a dank passageway, "the tomb of the dead".

The "Coffin-Worms"
follow and enter
the "room of disintegration".
A sepulchral voice asks,
"who is there?"
And the monk intones,
"a candidate for the grave".

The voice replies,
"then take your place
among the countless
millions who have
crossed into the
dreamless sleep."

As a harmonium wheezes off-key and funeral bells toll, a male corpse is seen in an upright coffin.

CABARET DU NÉANT - Paris-Montmartre — n° 3, Caveau des Trépassés

The "Worms" are quickly seated in the "Tomb of the Dead".

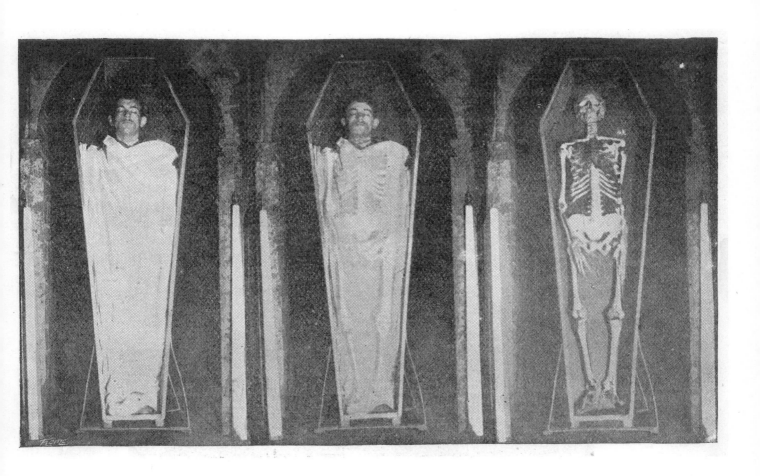

Where a body slowly rots away before their eyes.

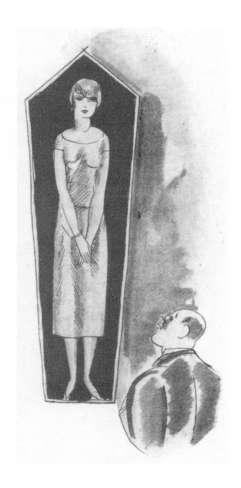

The next figure to appear in the coffin is a rosy-faced girl. She too decomposes into a bald and fleshless corpse.

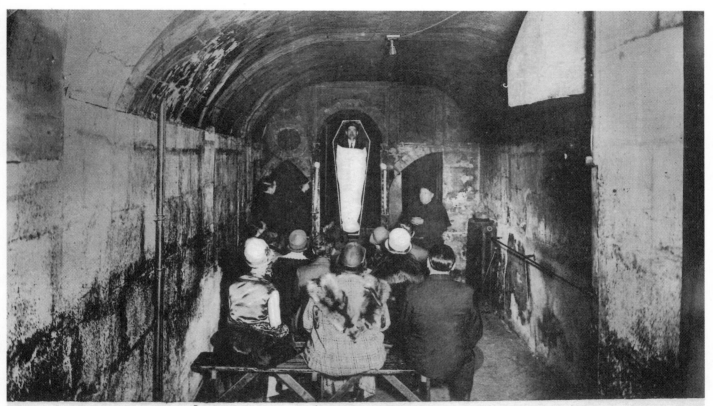

CABARET DU NÉANT - Paris-Montmartre - n° 3, Caveau des Trépassés - Première phase

Then a spectator is invited to stand in the coffin.

Cabaret du Néant - Paris-Montmartre — nº 4, Caveau des Trépassés, 2ᵉ phase — **B. F., PARIS**

In a flash, his body transforms into skeletal remains.

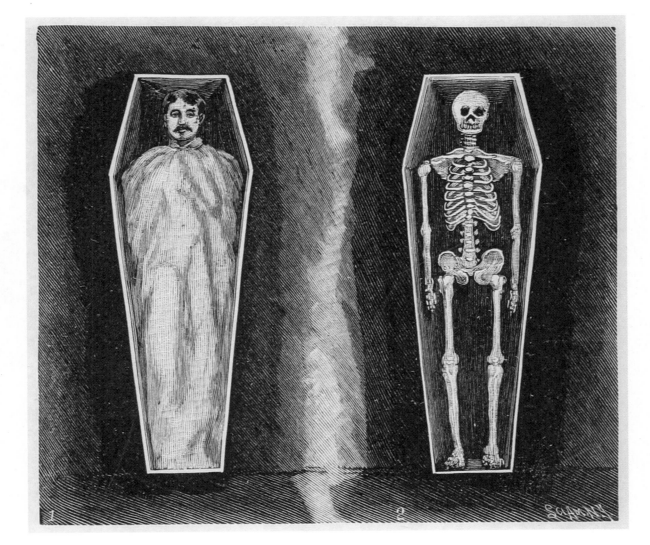

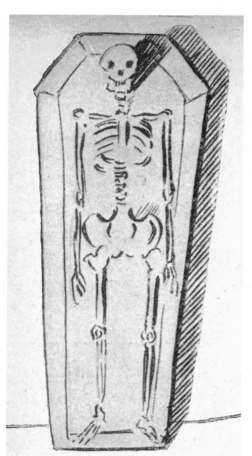

This startles the spectators.

All of these optical tricks are accomplished through mirrored projections, known as the "Pepper effect", or "Pepper's Ghost".

Cabaret du Néant — Paris-Montmartre — n° 5, Galerie des Spectres

For another franc, the "Coffin-Worms" are brought into a third room,
"The gallery of ghosts". There, an audience member is asked to sit on the stage.
Unseen by him, a ghoulish spirit materializes.

The mysterious phantom silently sets objects on an infant's coffin top.
To the shill, they are totally invisible. (Again, Pepper's Ghost.)

CABARET DU NÉANT - Paris-Montmartre --- nº 4. Caveau, Les Spectres gais

Now a sexy phantom girl teases our spectator.

She approaches him …

... *and seems to stroke his head and shoulders.*

Finally, a female spectator is called to the stage and a sad ghost retrieves a petrified rabbit from the coffin.
Then, without any warning, her outer garments vanish, and she is made to appear in some very provocative underclothing.
She is quite unconscious of this immodest proceeding. The expression of apprehensive astonishment with which
she stares at the audience—who are laughing in child-like delight—is worth the entire ten francs.

As the audience exits, they pass by an inscription. Then they are encouraged to drop some coins or bills into an inverted skull or hat, which will ensure them a prolonged life.

"Posthumous regret:
she died a virgin."

CABARET DE L'ENFER
& CABARET DU CIEL

CABARETS OF HELL & HEAVEN, PARIS, 1892–1950

In November 1892, a professor of literature, Antonin Alexander (known simply as Alexander) decided to install two competing cabarets kitty corner to the Cabaret du Néant, the Cabaret de l'Enfer and the Cabaret du Ciel (the Cabaret of Hell and the Cabaret of Heaven). Alexander's two restaurant-cabarets were equally profane but their mood was more jovial than frightening. Both had striking facades and costumed characters that goaded passers-by to experience the hellish or divine worlds-to-come. The professor conceived his side-by-side funhouses as a "stroll through Dante's Inferno."

At the Cabaret de l'Enfer, Alexander, who played the part of a leering and mustached Mephistopheles for several decades, wore an imperial red robe, adorned with sparkling jewels, and brandished a sword that emitted flames. The drinks there were considerably more expensive than the ones at the Cabaret du Ciel and the food much worse. Alexander explained, "Everything costs more in Hell because it's more fun. There are no rules here! Heaven is nothing but rules. My friends, where would you rather be?"

The upstairs play room, the "Hot Chamber," where nude angels swung from the ceiling and Pepper Effect reflections humiliated selected guests, was said to be the coldest enclosure in Montmartre. Monoprix, the Parisian grocery chain, purchased the two restaurants in 1950 and converted them to one mammoth luxury store, which still stands.

Image left: Cabaret de l'Enfer, Robert Doisneau, 1952.

CABARET DE L'ENFER

53, BOULEVARD DE CLICHY 1896–1950

AREA

9th ARRONDISSEMENT. Naturally, in the center of Montmartre.

ATMOSPHERE

The entrance to this cabaret artistique is framed with a gaping Hell's Mouth. A doorman dressed like an impish devil waves in potential clients. By his side is a placard that indicates the sweltering temperature inside, which is billed as "the most unique cabaret in the world." The pace indoors is fast moving and madly frantic.

CLIENTELE

Anglo-Saxon tourists mostly.

DÉCOR

An enormous bubbling caldron welcomes the guests to the depths of Purgatory on the ground floor. From a maze of cavern-like walls, thick clouds of smoke and crackling flames erupt. All the tables are topped with glass through which a red light streams. Snakes and serpents, pulled by strings, twist over the heads of the diners.

ENTERTAINMENT

A Gypsy band of male and female musicians bang out selections from *Faust* on guitars while devils prod the recalcitrant music-makers with tridents. After a black-mustached Mephisto and Lucifer roundly insult the diners, they are directed up a stairway to la Chaudière, or the "Hot Chamber."

EROTIC ENTICEMENT

In the cabaret, Satan introduces the audience to his diabolic spouse, whom he binds to a pillar as he spreads hell-fire around her feet. She is completely consumed in the flames. As soon as the smoke clears, a young female spectator is asked to repeat the auto-da-fé. But moments after the "eternally damned" femme is tied to the stake, the volunteer appears totally naked (through an optical illusion) and remains that way until the laughter ceases.

FOOD

Novelty drinks.

UNUSUAL

La Chaudière is actually the chilliest place in Pigalle.

The hell's mouth entrance has green eyes and is decked out in red and black.

CABARET DE L'ENFER

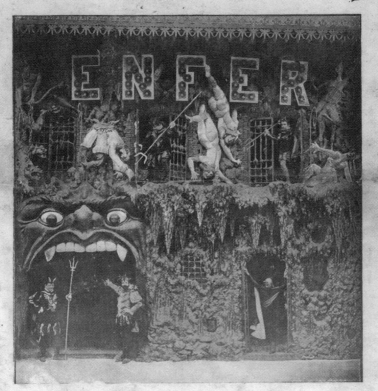

ENFER

53 · BOULEVARD DE CLICHY · 53
PARIS - MONTMARTRE

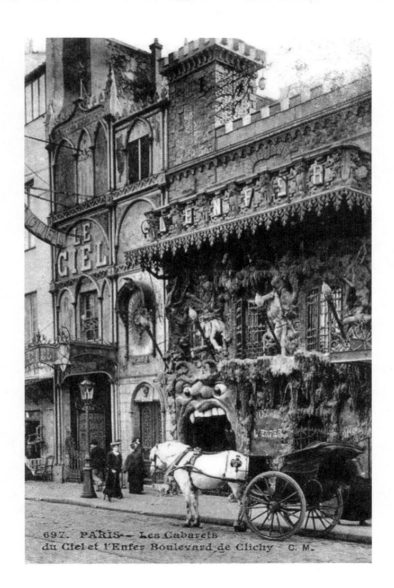

697. PARIS — Les Cabarets
du Ciel et l'Enfer Boulevard de Clichy   C. M.

A devil-like doorman in red calls out: "Enter and be damned! The evil one awaits you!"

A chorus of imps warn passers-by that they are "infernal sinners" and will be roasted both in this world and the next if they can help it.

A gendarme seats the "sinners" in "purgatory", a mock burning cavern where electric flames shoot from the walls and felt snakes dangle from the ceiling.

MONTMARTRE   "HELL"   PARIS

The most unique cabaret in the world open every evening at 8.30

PROGRAMME

PART I
(Ground floor)

Visitors purify their souls in Purgatory.

Their suffering is greatly mitigated by up to date music, dancing and 1ˢⁱ class Refreshments.

Discours by Lucifer and Satanas.

No extra charge is made for the entertainment on the floor above.

PART II
(1st floor)

Satan introduces his diabolic spouse Titania casts her into hell flames and her body is completely consumed in full wiew of all the spectators.

Any lady from the audience may maka the experiment.

Illustrations of the sufferings of the eternal damned and tableaux vivants of the deadly sins.

In "Lucifer's den", the waiter defies a "damned one" to order a "bumper of molten sin"
(a glass of bock beer) or a "swarm of sins with a pinch of sulpher" (coffee with a dash of cognac).

Mephistopheles lists the "seven deadly sins of eternal damnation" while an imp provides the diabolical drinks.

In the front cauldron, a Gypsy band of male and female "condemned souls" plays selections from Faust.

ORCHESTRE DIABOLIQUE

VUES PRISES A L'INTÉRIEUR DU CABARET

As the diabolical orchestra drones on, the red imps poke the "lost souls" with their tridents.

Lucifer describes the punishing qualities of each drink and dish: "That sausage will seal your intestines for twenty days!"

Lucifer (to a Female Sinner): Ah you! Why do you tremble? How many men have you sent hither to damnation with those beautiful eyes, those rosy tempting lips? Ah, for all that, you have found a sufficient hell on earth. But you, you will have the finest, the most exquisite tortures that await the damned. For what? For being a fool. It is folly more than crime that Hell punishes, for crime is a disease and folly a sin. You fool! For thus hanging upon the witching glance and oily words of a woman you have filled all Hell with fuel for your roasting. You will suffer such tortures as only the fool invites, such tortures only as are adequate to punish folly. Prepare for the inconceivable, the unimaginable, the things that even the King of Hell dare not mention lest the whole structure of damnation totter and crumble to dust.

Then *Lucifer* turns to a Male Sinner:

You do me great honor, sir. You may have been expecting to avoid me but reflect upon what you would have missed! We have many notables here, and you will have charming society. They do not include pickpockets and thieves, nor any others of the weak, stunted, crippled, and halting. You will find that most of your companions are distinguished gentlemen of learning and ability, who, knowing their duty, failed to perform it. You will be in excellent company, sir. To the Hot Room, all of you!

After Lucifer finishes his curses, the red imps torment one of their own in the back cauldron.

Finally, Mephistopheles (played by Alexander) proclaims, "hellfire approaches!"

Mephistopheles leads the sinners upstairs to the "hot chamber" of hell.

The upstairs entrance to the "hot chamber".

Satan holds a pack of Cerbères, the "watchdogs of hell".

VUES PRISES à L'INTERIEUR DU CABARET

TORTURE D'UN DAMNÉ

The torture of the damned …

… In their infernal toilet.

Satan introduces his consort Titania.

SUPLICE DES PECHERESSES

VUES PRISES A L'INTERIEUR DU CABARET

Titania is tied to a post.

The miserables grab the devil by the tail, while Titania is consumed in the flames of hellfire.

In the tribunal of hell,
Satan invites a male spectator
to ascend to the platform.

The "damned soul" sits,
facing the audience.

Unseen by him, Titania
strips off her toga and
walks to his side.
She makes carnal gestures
around his chair.

But he does not seem to notice
and is waved off the stage
to the hoots of the spectators.

Now a "damned" female volunteer
is brought to the platform.
Her body is suddenly engulfed
in crimson flames and
then magically reappears.
She too is rudely dismissed
and returns to her seat
in the house.

VUES PRISES A L'INTÉRIEUR DU CABARET.

LE TRIBUNAL DES ENFERS

The "horseman of death" arrives on a bicycle.

The gendarme brings down the curtain, promising to maintain "the sufferings of the eternally damned".

CABARET DU CIEL

53, BOULEVARD DE CLICHY 1896–1950

AREA

9th ARRONDISSEMENT. Next door to the Cabaret of Hell.

ATMOSPHERE

The mood is surprisingly solemn while noisy and bustling. Cold blue lights shine on a passageway of angels, gold-lined clouds, saints, sacred palms and other paraphernalia suggestive of St. Peter's kingdom.

CLIENTELE

Foreign tourists and some French families.

DÉCOR

On the ground floor, "Paradise," long white tables fill the center area. Above is a ceiling, designed to represent the higher stratospheres. In the back, an altar to a giant gilded pig and devotional candelabra rest against a wall. A dolorous church organ reverberates across the room. In the basement, a tiny auditorium, described as "Heaven," serves as a staging venue.

ENTERTAINMENT

While angelic dressed musicians strum wooden lyres and harps, a humorous preacher narrates "The Monk's Dream," a series of tableaux vivants that illustrate the many "lusts of the flesh."

EROTIC ENTICEMENT

Audience participation/humiliation, nudity, and optical illusions created with concealed mirrors. Customers descend from the cloistered dining hall and enter Heaven, where a female spectator metamorphoses into an angel. A second gyrating female angel flies about on a cord and tactically teases the most timid of the male spectators. Afterwards he is invited to a stage table and served a drink. What he cannot see is the naked hostess who brings him the glass and then expresses her indignation at his lack of interest.

FOOD

Verre de Chartreuse, called "the Star-Dazzler," is the house drink. Bock beer—"Heaven's Own Brew"—is also a favorite.

A guard beckons customers into the cabaret.

BOURGERIE & Cie PARIS

ENTRANCE TO "HEAVEN"

A plaster angel by the blue doorway welcomes the diners to paradise.

A "celestial banquet" on a communal table awaits the visitors.

While organs blast, the "garçons of heaven" seat the couples.

In the mock Gothic cathedral setting, Saint Peter and Saint Michael receive the guests.

CAFE DU CIEL.

They order drinks from the "garçons": "ambrosia of the gods" (champagne), "Heaven's own brew" (Alsatian bock beer),
"divine nectar" (cherries-in-brandy), or "star-dazzlers" (verre de charteuse).

MONTMARTRE — **"HEAVEN"** — PARIS

The leading artistic cabaret open every evening at 8.30

PROGRAMME

PART I

(Ground floor)

"PARADISE"

Divîne service and sermon by the most humorous preacher in Paris.

"THE MONK'S DREAM"

Illustrated by tableaux vivants of the lusts of the flesh.

I[st] class refreshments served during the spectacle.

No extra charge is made for the entertainment on the floor above.

PART II

(Ist floor)

"HEAVEN"

Suave visions of celestial bliss acrobatics by angels in the clouds.

Metamorphos of a lady spectator into an angel. Safe return to former condition ensured. Interesting experiments made with the assistance of gentlemen from the audience.

Visions of mahometan Paradise and oriental ecstasy.

Imp. Dupuy Jeune 74 Quai Jemmapes. Paris

Father Onésime, dressed in a velvet jerkin, sprinkles "the faithful" with holy water and recites his sermon, "the monk's dream".

Joséphine upends father Onésime's homily by cajoling the reverend into confessing his fleshly sins.

Joséphine then directs the rose-bedecked "seraphins" to kneel at the altar of Porcus, their "god of pleasure".

Saint Michael appears from "a cloud in the sky" and reminds the "faithful":
"Before you meet thy great creator, don't forget to tip your waiter".

Saint Michael delivers "the sermon of the golden calf".
At the conclusion, he invites the audience to leave "paradise"
and accompany him to "heaven" above.

*After accepting their one-franc jetons, the reverend guides the
spectators up the staircase to the second floor.*

St. Peter opens the upstairs portal with his "key to heaven"
and leads "the procession of the purified" to their seats.
An officer of the peace closes the door.

On the side of the grotto stage, Dante admonishes "the elect"
to avoid the "nine circles of hell".

Winged female angels in pink tights fly through the air in celestial bliss.

A male spectator is invited to sit on the stage, where he is erotically teased by an air-bound "Seraphin" that he cannot see. Finally, a female spectator replaces him and is transformed into a naked angel.

HIMMEL UND HÖLLE

HEAVEN AND HELL, BERLIN, 1924—1933

Himmel und Hölle (Heaven and Hell) in Berlin borrowed several elements from Alexander's original Cabaret de l'Enfer, mainly its liquor menu with a naked barmaid and elaborate nude performances. A Parisian choreographer, Madeleine Nervi, staged French-themed sketches, which varied from month to month.

When Himmel und Hölle opened on the Ku'damm in 1927, it attracted an unusually affluent crowd, including, one journalist crowed, "the longest legged women in the city." Although Berlin had countless burlesque-like cabarets and strip-joints during the 1920s, few enjoyed Himmel und Hölle's publicity and tabloid exposure. The freewheeling S/M shows were thought be the height of international sophistication.

Unlike Berlin's revue and variety theaters, the Himmel und Hölle could not survive the minute nips and cuts from the city's newly empowered censoring boards that fanned out in 1933. It was permanently closed by the Nazis that year.

Berlin spectators in 1931.

Tables by the bar.

The bar-maid serves "cherry cobblers" …   *… And then mixes a champagne "hell-cocktail" …*

… Concluding with a demonic stir.

Madeleine Nervi's girls open the show before a phallic tower.

"The Frenchwoman: Her Life Mirrored in Art" in "25 Naked Acts".

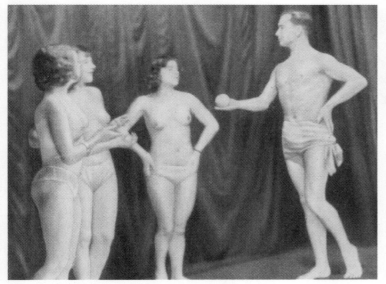

"The Judgment of Paris".

"Marquis de Sade in Hell: 25 Naked Pictures".

Enslavement.

A medieval execution.

The guillotine.

A funeral pyre.

THE CATACOMBS

OHIO, UNITED STATES, 1940—1941

Matchbook advertisement.

In August 1940, Albert Pick, Jr., a Chicago philanthropist and celebrated hotelman, opened a third commercial property in Columbus, Ohio, The Catacombs. This was an underground nightclub that mimicked the layout and contours of an ancient Roman burial gallery. *Life* magazine (September 23, 1940) heralded its unlikely thematic attraction and milieu in an extensive photo spread.

Columbus patrons stepped down a flight of stairs into a faux elevator that simulated a 300-foot drop into a corpse-filled vault. After experiencing that shaking mechanical descent, they were led by skeleton-clad guides (Ohio State University students) through dim, spider-webbed corridors, skull-lined rooms, and chambers of mummified bodies into a restaurant and dance hall.

Although the initial ambiance terrified some naive clients—with dripping stalactites and echoes of clanking chains and ghastly screams—its overall tongue-in-cheek atmosphere strongly resembled an Abbott and Costello horror film. Brooding guards roared and leaped behind guests as they passed by. In the "Nut House," saucy waitresses insulted the diners and spilled peanut shells in their laps. Dr. Marcus, a frenetic magician, sliced men's shirt sleeves and pulled guinea pigs and rabbits from their coat collars.

The horrific environment, interspersed with vaudevillian practical jokes, proved highly profitable for one year. The Catacombs was unexpectedly shuttered in July 1941.

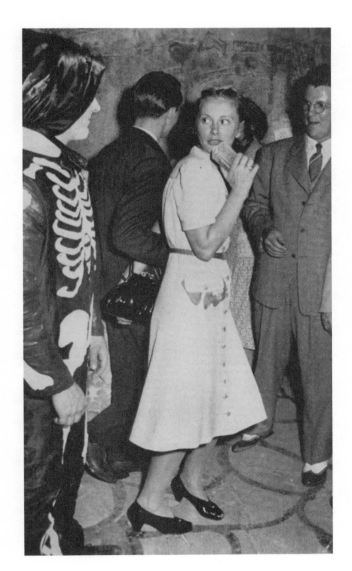

*A "living specter"
leads guests from
the elevator into
the catacombs.*

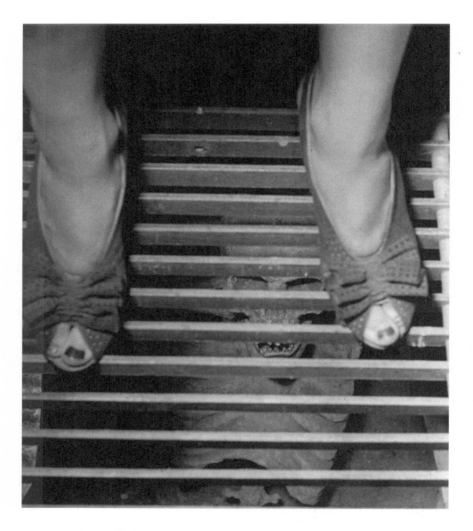

They walk down the stairs into "the tomb of the repentant sinner" …

… And the "chapel of a thousand skulls".

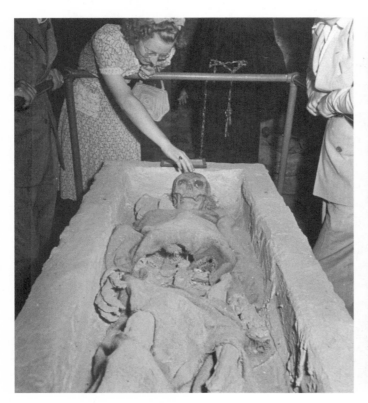

"The keeper of the tombs," who is ball-and-chained to a cadaver,
introduces "the guest of honor" to a line of curious patrons.

The "specter" displays two deceased friars.

Julius, the dead physician, shakes, giggles, and babbles away.

A customer inspects "mortuary row," which is lighted in an eerie green:
"Married couple: lived together, stuck together, died together."

In the dining hall, "the nut house," the cigarette-girl hawks cigarettes and skulls.

The sultry waitress insults the diners, tosses peanuts in their laps,
and yanks off their tablecloth.

Finally, Dr. Marcus,
a comic magician,
plucks a bunny
from a customer's suit…

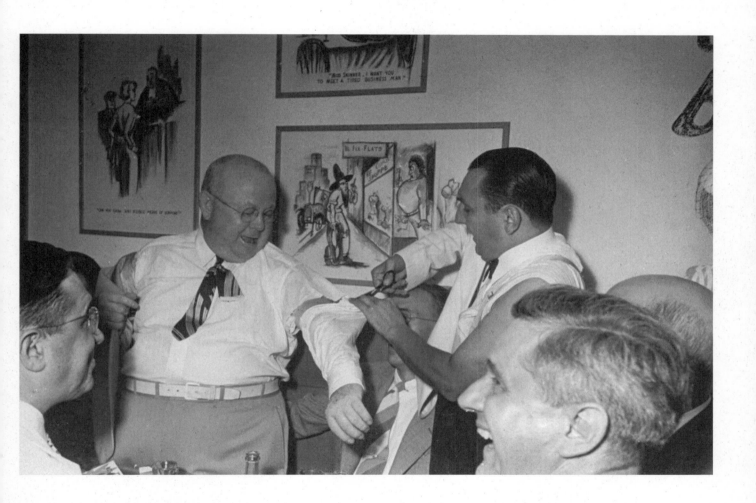

… And then slices the sleeve of a diner's shirt.

L'ENFER DE HEL

HE HELL OF HELL, BRUSSELS, 1955—195

Above: Entry to the club.

The last of the Cabarets of Death, L'Enfer de Hel (The Hell of Hell), was launched not far from the original Café de Mort in Brussels in 1955. Its name, a neologism of French and Flemish, like its humor, was distinctly working-class and lowbrow.

Among the hired help were bartenders and guides masked as grinning corpses and musicians in oversized rat costumes. Ashtrays and food bills sprang to life and beer steins were served in ceramic skulls.

A mechanical cow welcomed the diners to the "Chamber of Horrors" restaurant. There was a dance floor and a separate "Satan's Room," where couples could publicly cuddle and drink beer. The comic grotesque enterprise lasted for two years.

On the wall: "the dragon uses his magic to drag Hitler into hell."

A diner recoils from a bowl that flares up.

In the "chamber of horrors," a mechanical calf bellows.

A couple performs the "satanic shuffle" on the dance floor.

Another couple makes out in "Satan's room".

Later a team of wrestlers imbibe from skull mugs.

BIBLIOGRAPHY

John Chancellor, *How to Be Happy in Paris Without Being Ruined!* (London: Arrowsmith, 1926).

Mel Gordon, *Horizontal Collaboration: the Erotic World of Paris, 1920-1946* (Port Townsend, WA: Feral House, 2015).

C.R. Graham, *Roses and Thorns of Paris and London* (New York: n.p, 1897).

Albert A. Hopkins, *Magic: Stage Illusions and Scientific Diversions* (N.Y.: Munn & Co., 1898).

W.C. Morrow and Edouard Cucuel, *Bohemian Paris of To-Day* (Philadelphia & London: J.B. Lippincott, 1900).

Ralph Nevill, *Days and Nights in Montmartre and the Latin Quarter* (N.Y.: George H. Doran Co., 1927).

Pleasure Guide to Paris (Paris: Administration, 1923).

Roland Vale, *Night Haunts of Paris* (Hanley, UK: The Archer Press, 1949).

CONTEMPORARY REFERENCES

Cabaret du Ciel Program (1892).

Cabaret de L'Enfer Program (1895).

Cabaret du Néant Menu (1920).

Kriminal-Magazin #3 (June 1929) ("Das Cabaret du Néant").